D1189862

AN

INQUIRY

INTO

THE NATURE AND PROGRESS

OF

RENT,

AND THE

PRINCIPLES BY WHICH IT IS REGULATED.

―――――
―――――

BY

THE REV. T. R. MALTHUS,

*Professor of History and Political Economy in the East India College,
Hertfordshire.*

―――――
―――――

GREENWOOD PRESS, PUBLISHERS
NEW YORK

Originally published in 1815
by John Murray, London

First Greenwood Reprinting 1969

Library of Congress Catalogue Card Number 69-13984

SBN 8371-2362-3

PRINTED IN UNITED STATES OF AMERICA

ADVERTISEMENT.

The following Tract contains the substance of some notes on Rent, which, with others on different subjects relating to political economy, I have collected in the course of my professional duties at the East India College. It has been my intention, at some time or other, to put them in a form for publication; and the very near connexion of the subject of the present inquiry, with the topics immediately under discussion, has induced me to hasten its appearance at the present moment. It is the duty of those who have any means of contributing to the public stock of knowledge, not only to do so, but to do it at the time when it is most likely to be useful. If the nature of the disquisition should appear to the reader hardly to suit the form of a pamphlet, my apology must be, that it was not originally intended for so ephemeral a shape.

RENT, &c.

THE rent of land is a portion of the national revenue, which has always been considered as of very high importance.

According to Adam Smith, it is one of the three original sources of wealth, on which the three great divisions of society are supported.

By the Economists it is so pre-eminently distinguished, that it is considered as exclusively entitled to the name of riches, and the sole fund which is capable of supporting the taxes of the state, and on which they ultimately fall.

And it has, perhaps, a particular claim to our attention at the present moment, on account of the discussions which are going on respecting the Corn Laws, and the effects of rent on the price of raw produce, and the progress of agricultural improvement.

The rent of land may be defined to be that portion of the value of the whole produce which remains to the owner of the land, after all the outgoings belonging to its cultivation, of whatever kind, have been paid, including the profits of the capital employed, estimated according to the usual and ordinary rate of the profits of agricultural stock at the time being.

It sometimes happens, that from accidental and temporary circumstances, the farmer pays more, or less, than this; but this is the point towards which the actual rents paid are constantly gravitating, and which is therefore always referred to when the term is used in a general sense.

The immediate cause of rent is obviously the excess of price above the cost of production at which raw produce sells in the market.

The first object therefore which presents itself for inquiry, is the cause or causes of the high price of raw produce.

After very careful and repeated revisions of the subject, I do not find myself able to agree entirely in the view taken of it, either by Adam Smith, or the Economists; and still less, by some more modern writers.

Almost all these writers appear to me to consider rent as too nearly resembling in its nature, and the laws by which it is governed, the excess of price above the cost of production, which is the characteristic of a monopoly.

Adam Smith, though in some parts of the eleventh chapter of his first book he contemplates rent quite in its true light,* and has interspersed through his work more just observations on the subject than any other writer, has not explained the most essential cause of the high price of raw produce with sufficient distinctness, though he often touches on it; and by applying occasionally the term monopoly to the rent of land, without stopping to mark its more radical peculiarities, he leaves the reader without a definite impression of the real difference between the cause of the high price of the necessaries of life, and of monopolized commodities.

Some of the views which the Economists have taken of the nature of rent appear to me, in like manner, to be quite just; but they have mixed them with so much error, and have drawn such preposterous and contradictory conclusions from them, that what is true in

---

* I cannot, however, agree with him in thinking that all land which yields food must necessarily yield rent. The land which is successively taken into cultivation in improving countries, may only pay profits and labour. A fair profit on the stock employed, including, of course, the payment of labour, will always be a sufficient inducement to cultivate.

their doctrines, has been obscured and lost in the mass of superincumbent error, and has in consequence produced little effect. Their great practical conclusion, namely, the propriety of taxing exclusively the neat rents of the landlords, evidently depends upon their considering these rents as completely disposeable, like that excess of price above the cost of production which distinguishes a common monopoly.

Mr. Say, in his valuable Treatise on Political Economy, in which he has explained with great clearness many points which have not been sufficiently developed by Adam Smith, has not treated the subject of rent in a manner entirely satisfactory. In speaking of the different natural agents which, as well as the land, co-operate with the labours of man, he observes: " Heureusement personne n'a pu dire le vent et le soleil m'appartiennent, et le service qu'ils rendent doit m'etre payè."* And, though he acknowledges that, for obvious reasons, property in land is necessary, yet he evidently considers rent as almost exclusively owing

---

* Vol. II. p. 124. Of this work a new and much improved edition has lately been published, which is highly worthy the attention of all those who take an interest in these subjects.

to such appropriation, and to external demand.

In the excellent work of M. de Sismondi, *De la Richesse Commerciale*, he says in a note on the subject of rent: "Cette partie de la rente foncière est celle que les Economistes ont decorée du nom du *produit net* comme étant le seul fruit du travail qui ajoutât quelque chore a la richesse nationale. On pourroit au contraire soutenir contre eux, que c'est la seule partie du produit du travail, dont la valeur soit purement nominale, et n'ait rien de réelle: c'est en effet le resultat de l'augmentation de prix qu'obtient un vendeur en vèrtu de son privilege, sans que la chose vendue en vaille rèellement d'avantage."*

The prevailing opinions among the more modern writers in our own country, have appeared to me to incline towards a similar view of the subject; and, not to multiply citations, I shall only add, that in a very respectable edition of the *Wealth of Nations*, lately published by Mr. Buchanan, of Edinburgh, the idea of monopoly is pushed still farther. And while former writers, though they considered rent as governed by the laws of monopoly, were still of opinion that this monopoly in the case of

* Vol. I. p. 49.

land was necessary and useful, Mr. Buchanan sometimes speaks of it even as prejudicial, and as depriving the consumer of what it gives to the landlord.

In treating of productive and unproductive labour in the last volume, he observes,* that, "The neat surplus by which the Economists estimate the utility of agriculture, plainly arises from the high price of its produce, which, however advantageous to the landlord who receives it, is surely no advantage to the consumer who pays it. Were the produce of agriculture to be sold for a lower price, the same neat surplus would not remain, after defraying the expenses of cultivation; but agriculture would be still equally productive to the general stock; and the only difference would be, that as the landlord was formerly enriched by the high price, at the expense of the community, the community would now profit by the low price at the expense of the landlord. The high price in which the rent or neat surplus originates, while it enriches the landlord who has the produce of agriculture to sell, diminishes in the same proportion the wealth of those who are its purchasers; and on this account it is quite inaccurate to consider the landlord's rent as a clear addition to the national wealth." In other parts of his work he uses the same, or even stronger language, and in a note on the subject of taxes, he speaks of the high price of the produce of land as advantageous to those who receive it, but proportionably *injurious* to those who pay it. " In this view," he adds, " it can form no general addition to the stock of the community, as the neat surplus in question is nothing more than a revenue transferred from one class to another, and from the mere circumstance of its thus changing hands, it is clear that no fund can arise out of which to pay taxes. The revenue which pays for the produce of land exists already in the hands of those who purchase that produce; and, if the price of subsistence were lower, it would still remain in their hands, where it would be just as available for taxation, as when by a higher price it is transferred to the landed proprietor."*

That there are some circumstances connected with rent, which have an affinity to a natural monopoly, will he readily allowed. The extent of the earth itself is limited, and cannot be enlarged by human demand. And the inequality of soils occasions, even at an early period of society, a comparative scarcity of the best lands ; and so far is undoubtedly one of the causes of rent properly so called. On this account, perhaps, the term *partial monopoly* might be fairly applicable. But the scarcity of land, thus implied, is by no means alone sufficient to produce the effects observed. And a more accurate investigation of the subject will shew us how essentially different the high price of raw produce is, both in its nature and origin, and the laws by which it is governed, from the high price of a common monopoly.

The causes of the high price of raw produce may be stated to be three.

First, and mainly, That quality of the earth, by which it can be made to yield a greater portion of the necessaries of life than is required for the maintenance of the persons employed on the land.

2dly, That quality peculiar to the necessaries of life of being able to create their own demand, or to raise up a number of demanders in proportion to the quantity of necessaries produced.

And, 3dly, The comparative scarcity of the most fertile land.

The qualities of the soil and of its products, here noticed as the primary causes of the high price of raw produce, are the gifts of nature to man. They are quite unconnected with monopoly, and yet are so absolutely essential to the existence of rent, that without them, no degree of scarcity or monopoly could have occasioned that excess of the price of raw produce, above the cost of production, which shews itself in this form.

If, for instance, the soil of the earth had been such, that, however well directed might have been the industry of man, he could not have produced from it more than was barely sufficient to maintain those, whose labour and attention were necessary to its products; though, in this case, food and raw materials would have been evidently scarcer than at present, and the land might have been, in the same manner, monopolized by particular owners; yet it is quite clear, that neither rent, nor any essential surplus produce of the land in the form of high profits, could have existed.

It is equally clear, that if the necessaries of life—the most important products of land, had not the property of creating an increase of demand proportioned to their increased quantity, such increased quantity would occasion a fall in their exchangeable value. However abundant might be the produce of a country, its population might remain stationary. And this abundance, without a proportionate demand,

and with a very high corn-price of labour, which would naturally take place under these circumstances, might reduce the price of raw produce, like the price of manufactures, to the cost of production.

It has been sometimes argued, that it is mistaking the principle of population, to imagine, that the increase of food, or of raw produce alone, can occasion a proportionate increase of population. This is no doubt true; but it must be allowed, as has been justly observed by Adam Smith, that "when food is provided, it is comparatively easy to find the necessary clothing and lodging." And it should always be recollected, that land does not produce one commodity alone, but in addition to that most indispensable of all commodities—food, it produces also the materials for the other necessaries of life; and the labour required to work up these materials is of course never excluded from the consideration.*

---

* It is, however, certain, that if either these materials be wanting, or the skill and capital necessary to work them up be prevented from forming, owing to the insecurity of property, or any other cause, the cultivators will soon slacken in their exertions, and the motives to accumulate and to increase their produce, will greatly diminish. But in this case there will be a very slack demand for labour; and, whatever

It is, therefore, strictly true, that land produces the necessaries of life,—produces food, materials, and labour,—produces the means by which, and by which alone, an increase of people may be brought into being, and supported. In this respect it is fundamentally different from every other kind of machine known to man; and it is natural to suppose, that it should be attended with some peculiar effects.

If the cotton machinery, in this country, were to go on increasing at its present rate, or even much faster; but instead of producing one particular sort of substance which may be used for some parts of dress and furniture, &c. had the qualities of land, and could yield what, with the assistance of a little labour, economy, and skill, could furnish food, clothing, and lodging, in such proportions as to create an increase of population equal to the increased supply of these necessaries ; the demand for the products of such improved machinery would continue in excess above the cost of production, and this excess would no

---

may be the nominal cheapness of provisions, the labourer will not really be able to command such a portion of the necessaries of life, including, of course, clothing, lodging, &c. as will occasion an increase of population.

longer exclusively belong to the machinery of the land.*

There is a radical difference in the cause of a demand for those objects which are strictly necessary to the support of human life, and a demand for all other commodities. In all other commodities the demand is exterior to, and independent of, the production itself; and in the case of a monopoly, whether natural or artificial, the excess of price is in proportion to the smallness of the supply compared with the demand, while this demand is comparatively unlimited. In the case of strict necessaries, the existence and increase of the demand, or of the number of demanders, must depend upon the existence and increase of these necessaries themselves; and the excess of their price above the cost of their production must depend upon, and is permanently limited by, the excess of their quantity above the quantity necessary to maintain the labour required to produce them; without which excess of quantity no demand could have existed,

---

* I have supposed some check to the supply of the cotton machinery in this case. If there was no check whatever, the effects would shew themselves in excessive profits and excessive wages, without an excess above the cost of production.

according to the laws of nature, for more than was necessary to support the producers.

It has been stated, in the new edition of the " *Wealth of Nations*," that the cause of the high price of raw produce is, that such price is required to proportion the consumption to the supply.* This is also true, but it affords no solution of the point in question. We still want to know why the consumption and supply are such as to make the price so greatly exceed the cost of production, and the main cause is evidently the *fertility* of the earth in producing the necessaries of life. Diminish this plenty, diminish the fertility of the soil, and the excess will diminish; diminish it still further, and it will disappear. The cause of the high price of the necessaries of life above the cost of production, is to be found in their abundance, rather than their scarcity; and is not only essentially different from the high price occasioned by artificial monopolies, but from the high price of those peculiar products of the earth, not connected with food, which may be called natural and necessary monopolies.

The produce of certain vineyards in France, which, from the peculiarity of their soil and situation, exclusively yield wine of a certain flavour, is sold of course at a price very far exceeding the cost of production. And this is owing to the greatness of the competition for such wine, compared with the scantiness of its supply; which confines the use of it to so small a number of persons, that they are able, and rather than go without it, willing, to give an excessively high price. But if the fertility of these lands were increased, so as very considerably to increase the produce, this produce might so fall in value as to diminish most essentially the excess of its price above the cost of production. While, on the other hand, if the vineyards were to become less productive, this excess might increase to almost any extent.

The obvious cause of these effects is, that in all monopolies, properly so called, whether natural or artificial, the demand is exterior to, and independent of, the production itself. The number of persons who might have a taste for scarce wines, and would be desirous of entering into a competition for the purchase of them, might increase almost indefinitely, while the produce itself was decreasing; and its price, therefore, would have no other limit than the numbers, powers, and caprices, of the competitors for it.

In the production of the necessaries of life,
on the contrary, the demand is dependent upon
the produce itself; and the effects are, in consequence, widely different. In this case, it is
physically impossible that the number of demanders should increase, while the quantity of
produce diminishes, as the demanders only
exist by means of this produce. The fertility
of soil, and consequent abundance of produce
from a certain quantity of land, which, in the
former case, diminished the excess of price
above the cost of production, is, in the present
case, the specific cause of such excess; and the
diminished fertility, which in the former case
might increase the price to almost any excess
above the cost of production, may be safely
asserted to be the sole cause which could permanently maintain the necessaries of life at a
price not exceeding the cost of production.

Is it, then, possible to consider the price of
the necessaries of life as regulated upon the
principle of a common monopoly? Is it possible, with M. de Sismondi, to regard rent as
the sole produce of labour, which has a value
purely nominal, and the mere result of that
augmentation of price which a seller obtains
in consequence of a peculiar privilege: or, with
Mr. Buchanan, to consider it as no addition
to the national wealth, but merely as a trans-

fer of value, advantageous only to the landlords, and proportionably *injurious* to the consumers?

Is it not, on the contrary, a clear indica-
tion of a most inestimable quality in the soil,
which God has bestowed on man—the quality of being able to maintain more persons
than are necessary to work it. Is it not a part,
and we shall see further on that it is an absolutely necessary part, of that surplus produce
from the land,* which has been justly stated to
be the source of all power and enjoyment; and
without which, in fact, there would be no
cities, no military or naval force, no arts, no
learning, none of the finer manufactures, none
of the conveniences and luxuries of foreign
countries, and none of that cultivated and po-
lished society, which not only elevates and
dignifies individuals, but which extends its

---

* The more general surplus here alluded to is meant to
include the profits of the farmer, as well as the rents of the
landlord; and, therefore, includes the whole fund for the
support of those who are not directly employed upon the
land. Profits are, in reality, a surplus, as they are in no
respect proportioned (as intimated by the Economists) to
the wants and necessities of the owners of capital. But
they take a different course in the progress of society from
rents, and it is necessary, in general, to keep them quite
separate.

beneficial influence through the whole mass of the people?

In the early periods of society, or more remarkably perhaps, when the knowledge and capital of an old society are employed upon fresh and fertile land, this surplus produce, this bountiful gift of Providence, shews itself chiefly in extraordinary high profits, and extraordinary high wages, and appears but little in the shape of rent. While fertile land is in abundance, and may be had by whoever asks for it, nobody of course will pay a rent to a landlord. But it is not consistent with the laws of nature, and the limits and quality of the earth, that this state of things should continue. Diversities of soil and situation must necessarily exist in all countries. All land cannot be the most fertile: all situations cannot be the nearest to navigable rivers and markets. But the accumulation of capital beyond the means of employing it on land of the greatest natural fertility, and the greatest advantage of situation, must necessarily lower profits; while the tendency of population to increase beyond the means of subsistence must, after a certain time, lower the wages of labour.

The expense of production will thus be diminished, but the value of the produce, that is, the quantity of labour, and of the other products of labour besides corn, which it can command, instead of diminishing, will be increased. There will be an increasing number of people demanding subsistence, and ready to offer their services in any way in which they can be useful. The exchangeable value of food will, therefore, be in excess above the cost of production, including in this cost the full profits of the stock employed upon the land, according to the actual rate of profits, at the time being. And this excess is rent.

Nor is it possible that these rents should permanently remain as parts of the profits of stock, or of the wages of labour. If such an accumulation were to take place, as decidedly to lower the general profits of stock, and, consequently, the expenses of cultivation, so as to make it answer to cultivate poorer land; the cultivators of the richer land, if they paid no rent, would cease to be mere farmers, or persons living upon the profits of agricultural stock. They would unite the characters of farmers and landlords,—a union by no means uncommon; but which does not alter, in any degree, the nature of rent, or its essential separation from profits. If the general profits of stock were 20 per cent. and particular portions of land would yield 30 per cent. on the capital employed, 10 per cent. of the 30 would obviously be rent, by whomsoever received.

It happens, indeed, sometimes, that from bad government, extravagant habits, and a faulty constitution of society, the accumulation of capital is stopped, while fertile land is in considerable plenty, in which case profits may continue permanently very high; but even in this case wages must necessarily fall, which by reducing the expenses of cultivation must occasion rents. There is nothing so absolutely unavoidable in the progress of society as the fall of wages, that is such a fall as, combined with the habits of the labouring classes, will regulate the progress of population according to the means of subsistence. And when, from the want of an increase of capital, the increase of produce is checked, and the means of subsistence come to a stand, the wages of labour must necessarily fall so low, as only just to maintain the existing population, and to prevent any increase.

We observe in consequence, that in all those countries, such as Poland, where, from the want of accumulation, the profits of stock remain very high, and the progress of cultivation either proceeds very slowly, or is entirely stopped, the wages of labour are extremely low. And this cheapness of labour, by diminishing the expenses of cultivation, as far as labour is concerned, counteracts the effects of the high profits of stock, and generally leaves a larger rent to the landlord than in those countries, such as America, where, by a rapid accumulation of stock, which can still find advantageous employment, and a great demand for labour, which is accompanied by an adequate increase of produce and population, profits cannot be low, and labour for some considerable time remains very high.

It may be laid down, therefore, as an incontrovertible truth, that as a nation reaches any considerable degree of wealth, and any considerable fullness of population, which of course cannot take place without a great fall both in the profits of stock and the wages of labour, the separation of rents, as a kind of fixture upon lands of a certain quality, is a law as invariable as the action of the principle of gravity. And that rents are neither a mere nominal value, nor a value unnecessarily and injuriously transferred from one set of people to another; but a most real and essential part of the whole value of the national property, and placed by the laws of nature where they are, on the land, by whomsoever possessed, whether the landlord, the crown, or the actual cultivator.

Rent then has been traced to the same common nature with that general surplus from the land, which is the result of certain qualities of the soil and its products; and it has been found to commence its separation from profits, as soon as profits and wages fall, owing to the comparative scarcity of fertile land in the natural progress of a country towards wealth and population.

Having examined the nature and origin of rent, it remains for us to consider the laws by which it is governed, and by which its increase or decrease is regulated.

When capital has accumulated, and labour fallen on the most eligible lands of a country, other lands less favourably circumstanced with respect to fertility or situation, may be occupied with advantage. The expenses of cultivation, including profits, having fallen, poorer land, or land more distant from markets, though yielding at first no rent, may fully repay these expenses, and fully answer to the cultivator. And again, when either the profits of stock or the wages of labour, or both, have still further fallen, land still poorer, or still less favourably situated, may be taken into cultivation. And, at every step, it is clear, that if the price of produce does not fall, the rents of land will rise. And the price of produce will not fall, as long as the industry and ingenuity of the labouring classes, assisted by the capitals of

those not employed upon the land, can find
something to give in exchange to the cultivators
and landlords, which will stimulate them to
continue undiminished their agricultural exertions, and maintain their increasing excess of
produce.

In tracing more particularly the laws which
govern the rise and fall of rents, the main causes
which diminish the expenses of cultivation, or
reduce the cost of the instruments of production, compared with the price of produce, require to be more specifically enumerated. The
principal of these seem to be four:—1st, Such
an accumulation of capital as will lower the
profits of stock; 2dly, such an increase of
population as will lower the wages of labour;
3dly, such agricultural improvements, or such
increase of exertions, as will diminish the
number of labourers necessary to produce a
given effect; and 4thly, such an increase in
the price of agricultural produce, from increased demand, as without nominally lowering the expense of production, will increase
the difference between this expense and the
price of produce.

The operation of the three first causes in
lowering the expenses of cultivation, compared
with the price of produce, are quite obvious;
the fourth requires a few further observations.

If a great and continued demand should arise among surrounding nations for the raw produce of a particular country, the price of this produce would of course rise considerably; and the expenses of cultivation, rising only slowly and gradually to the same proportion, the price of produce might for a long time keep so much a head, as to give a prodigious stimulus to improvement, and encourage the employment of much capital in bringing fresh land under cultivation, and rendering the old much more productive.

Nor would the effect be essentially different in a country which continued to feed its own people, if instead of a demand for its raw produce, there was the same increasing demand for its manufactures. These manufactures, if from such a demand the value of their amount in foreign countries was greatly to increase, would bring back a great increase of value in return, which increase of value could not fail to increase the value of the raw produce. The demand for agricultural as well as manufactured produce would be augmented; and a considerable stimulus, though not perhaps to the same extent as in the last case, would be given to every kind of improvement on the land.

A similar effect would be produced by the

introduction of new machinery, and a more ju-
dicious division of labour in manufactures. It
almost always happens in this case, not only
that the quantity of manufactures is very
greatly increased, but that the value of the
whole mass is augmented, from the great extension of the demand for them, occasioned
by their cheapness. We see, in consequence,
that in all rich manufacturing and commercial
countries, the value of manufactured and commercial products bears a very high proportion
to the raw products ;* whereas, in comparatively poor countries, without much internal
trade and foreign commerce, the value of their
raw produce constitutes almost the whole of
their wealth. If we suppose the wages of
labour so to rise with the rise of produce, as to
give the labourer the same command of the
means of subsistence as before, yet if he is able
to purchase a greater quantity of other necessaries and conveniencies, both foreign and do-

---

* According to the calculations of Mr. Colquhoun, the
value of our trade, foreign and domestic, and of our manufactures, exclusive of raw materials, is nearly equal to the
gross value derived from the land. In no other large country probably is this the case.—Treatise on the Wealth,
Power, and Resources of the British Empire. p. 96. The
whole annual produce is estimated at about 430 millions, and
the products of agriculture at about 216 millions.

mestic, with the price of a given quantity of corn, he may be equally well fed, clothed, and lodged, and population may be equally encouraged, although the wages of labour may not rise so high in proportion as the price-of produce.

And even when the price of labour does really rise in proportion to the price of produce, which is a very rare case, and can only happen when the demand for labour precedes, or is at least quite contemporary with the demand for produce; it is so impossible that all the other outgoings in which capital is expended, should rise precisely in the same proportion, and at the same time, such as compositions for tithes, parish rates, taxes, manure, and the fixed capital accumulated under the former low prices, that a period of some continuance can scarcely fail to occur, when the difference between the price of produce and the cost of production is increased.

In some of these cases, the increase in the price of agricultural produce, compared with the cost of the instruments of production, appears from what has been said to be only temporary; and in these instances it will often give a considerable stimulus to cultivation, by an increase of agricultural profits, without shewing itself much in the shape of rent. It hardly ever fails, however, to increase rent ultimately. The increased capital, which is employed in consequence of the opportunity of making great temporary profits, can seldom or ever be entirely removed from the land, at the expiration of the current leases; and, on the renewal of these leases, the landlord feels the benefit of it in the increase of his rents.

Whenever then, by the operation of the four causes above mentioned, the difference between the price of produce and the cost of the instruments of production increases, the rents of land will rise.

It is, however, not necessary that all these four causes should operate at the same time; it is only necessary that the difference here mentioned should increase. If, for instance, the price of produce were to rise, while the wages of labour, and the price of the other branches of capital did not rise in proportion, and at the same time improved modes of agriculture were coming into general use, it is evident that this difference might be increased, although the profits of agricultural stock were not only undiminished, but were to rise decidedly higher.

Of the great additional quantity of capital employed upon the land in this country, during the last twenty years, by far the greater part is supposed to have been generated on the soil, and not to have been brought from commerce or manufactures. And it was unquestionably the high profits of agricultural stock, occasioned by improvements in the modes of agriculture, and by the constant rise of prices, followed only slowly by a proportionate rise in the different branches of capital, that afforded the means of so rapid and so advantageous an accumulation.

In this case cultivation has been extended, and rents have risen, although one of the instruments of production, capital, has been dearer.

In the same manner a fall of profits and improvements in agriculture, or even one of them separately, might raise rents, notwithstanding a rise of wages.

It may be laid down then as a general truth, that rents naturally rise as the difference between the price of produce and the cost of the instruments of production increases.

It is further evident, that no fresh land can be taken into cultivation till rents have risen, or would allow of a rise upon what is already cultivated.

Land of an inferior quality requires a great quantity of capital to make it yield a given produce; and, if the actual price of this produce be not such as fully to compensate the cost of production, including the existing rate of profits, the land must remain uncultivated. It matters not whether this compensation is effected by an increase in the money price of raw produce, without a proportionate increase in the money price of the instruments of production, or by a decrease in the price of the instruments of production, without a proportionate decrease in the price of produce. What is absolutely necessary, is a greater *relative* cheapness of the instruments of production, to make up for the quantity of them required to obtain a given produce from poor land.

But whenever, by the operation of one or more of the causes before mentioned, the instruments of production become cheaper, and the difference between the price of produce and the expenses of cultivation increases, rents naturally rise. It follows therefore as a direct and necessary consequence, that it can never answer to take fresh land of a poorer quality into cultivation, till rents have risen or would allow of a rise, on what is already cultivated.

It is equally true, that without the same tendency to a rise of rents, occasioned by the operation of the same causes, it cannot answer to lay out fresh capital in the improvement of old land,—at least upon the supposition, that each farm is already furnished with as much capital as can be laid out to advantage, according to the actual rate of profits.

It is only necessary to state this proposition to make its truth appear. It certainly may happen, and I fear it happens frequently, that farmers are not provided with all the capital which could be employed upon their farms, at the actual rate of agricultural profits. But supposing they are so provided, it implies distinctly, that more could not be applied without loss, till, by the operation of one or more of the causes above enumerated, rents had tended to rise.

It appears then, that the power of extending cultivation and increasing produce, both by the cultivation of fresh land and the improvement of the old, depends entirely upon the existence of such prices, compared with the expense of production, as would raise rents in the actual state of cultivation.

But though cultivation cannot be extended, and the produce of the country increased, but in such a state of things as would allow of a rise of rents, yet it is of importance to remark, that this rise of rents will be by no means in proportion to the extension of cultivation, or

the increase of produce. Every relative fall in
the price of the instruments of production,
may allow of the employment of a considerable
quantity of additional capital; and when either
new land is taken into cultivation, or the old
improved, the increase of produce may be considerable, though the increase of rents be trifling.
We see, in consequence, that in the progress
of a country towards a high state of cultivation, the quantity of capital employed upon
the land. and the quantity of produce yielded
by it, bears a constantly increasing proportion
to the amount of rents, unless counterbalanced
by extraordinary improvements in the modes
of cultivation.*

According to the returns lately made to the
Board of Agriculture, the average proportion
which rent bears to the value of the whole

---

* To the honour of Scotch cultivators, it should be observed, that they have applied their capitals so very skilfully
and economically, that at the same time that they have pro-
digiously increased the produce, they have increased the
landlord's proportion of it. The difference between the landlord's share of the produce in Scotland and in England is
quite extraordinary—much greater than can be accounted
for, either by the natural soil or the absence of tithes and
poors rates.—See Sir John Sinclair's valuable Account of
the Husbandry of Scotland; and the General Report not long
since published—works replete with the most useful and
interesting information on agricultural subjects.

produce, seems not to exceed one fifth;*
whereas formerly, when there was less capital
employed, and less value produced, the proportion amounted to one fourth, one third, or
even two fifths. Still, however, the numerical
difference between the price of produce and
the expenses of cultivation, increases with the
progress of improvement; and though the
landlord has a less *share* of the whole produce, yet this less share, from the very great
increase of the produce, yields a larger quantity, and gives him a greater command of corn
and labour. If the produce of land be represented by the number six, and the landlord
has one-fourth of it, his share will be represented
by one and a half. If the produce of land be
as ten, and the landlord has one-fifth of it, his
share will be represented by two. In the
latter case, therefore, though the proportion of
the landlord's share to the whole produce is
greatly diminished, his real rent, independently
of nominal price, will be increased in the proportion of from three to four. And in general,
in all cases of increasing produce, if the landlord's share of this produce do not diminish
in the same proportion, which though it often

---

* See Evidence before the House of Lords, given in by

happens during the currency of leases, rarely or never happens on the renewal of them, the real rents of land must rise.

We see then, that a progressive rise of rents seems to be necessarily connected with the progressive cultivation of new land, and the progressive improvement of the old : and that this rise is the natural and necessary consequence of the operation of four causes, which are the most certain indications of increasing prosperity and wealth—namely, the accumulation of capital, the increase of population, improvements in agriculture, and the high price of raw produce, occasioned by the extension of our manufactures and commerce.

On the other hand, it will appear, that a fall of rents is as necessarily connected with the throwing of inferior land out of cultivation, and the continued deterioration of the land of a superior quality; and that it is the natural and necessary consequence of causes, which are the certain indications of poverty and decline, namely, diminished capital, diminished population, a bad system of cultivation, and the low price of raw produce.

If it be true, that cultivation cannot be extended but under such a state of prices, compared with the expenses of production, as will allow of an increase of rents, it follows naturally that under such a state of relative prices as will occasion a fall of rents, cultivation must decline. If the instruments of production become dearer, compared with the price of produce, it is a certain sign that they are relatively scarce; and in all those cases where a large quantity of them is required, as in the cultivation of poor land, the means of procuring them will be deficient, and the land will be thrown out of employment.

It appeared, that in the progress of cultivation and of increasing rents, it was not necessary that all the instruments of production should fall in price at the same time; and that the difference between the price of produce and the expense of cultivation might increase, although either the profits of stock or the wages of labour might be higher, instead of lower.

In the same manner, when the produce of a country is declining, and rents are falling, it is not necessary that all the instruments of production should be dearer. In a declining or stationary country, one most important instrument of production is always cheap, namely, labour; but this cheapness of labour does not counterbalance the disadvantages arising from the dearness of capital; a bad system of culture; and, above all, a fall in the price of raw produce, greater than in the price of the other branches of expenditure, which, in addition to labour, are necessary to cultivation.

It has appeared also, that in the progress of cultivation and of increasing rents, rent, though greater in positive amount, bears a less, and lesser proportion to the quantity of capital employed upon the land, and the quantity of produce derived from it. According to the same principle, when produce diminishes and rents fall, though the amount of rent will always be less, the proportion which it bears to capital and produce will always be greater. And, as in the former case, the diminished proportion of rent was owing to the necessity of yearly taking fresh land of an inferior quality into cultivation, and proceeding in the improvement of old land, when it would return only the common profits of stock, with little or no rent; so, in the latter case, the high proportion of rent is owing to the impossibility of obtaining produce, whenever a great expenditure is required, and the necessity of employing the reduced capital of the country, in the exclusive cultivation of its richest lands.

In proportion, therefore, as the relative state of prices is such as to occasion a progressive fall of rents, more and more lands will be gradually thrown out of cultivation, the remainder will be worse cultivated, and the diminution of produce will proceed still faster than the diminution of rents.

If the doctrine here laid down, respecting the laws which govern the rise and fall of rents, be near the truth, the doctrine which maintains that, if the produce of agriculture were sold at such a price as to yield less neat surplus, agriculture would be equally productive to the general stock, must be very far from the truth.

With regard to my own conviction, indeed, I feel no sort of doubt that if, under the impression that the high price of raw produce, which occasions rent, is as injurious to the consumer as it is advantageous to the landlord, a rich and improved nation were determined by law, to lower the price of produce, till no surplus in the shape of rent any where remained; it would inevitably throw not only all the poor land, but all, except the very best land, out of cultivation, and probably reduce its produce and population to less than onetenth of their former amount.

From the preceding account of the progress of rent, it follows, that the actual state of the natural rent of land is necessary to the actual produce; and that the price of produce, in every progressive country, must be just about equal to the cost of production on land of the poorest quality actually in use; or to the cost of raising additional produce on old land, which yields only the usual returns of agricultural stock with little or no rent.

It is quite obvious that the price cannot be less ; or such land would not be cultivated, nor such capitai employed. Nor can it ever much exceed this price, because the poor land progressively taken into cultivation, yields at first little or no rent; and because it will always answer to any farmer who can command capital, to lay it out on his land, if the additional produce resulting from it will fully repay the profits of his stock, although it yields nothing to his landlord.

It follows then, that the price of raw produce, in reference to the *whole quantity* raised, is sold at the natural or necessary price, that is, at the price necessary to obtain the actual amount of produce, although by far the largest part is sold at a price very much above that which is necessary to its production, owing to this part being produced at less expense, while its exchangeable value remains undiminished.

The difference between the price of corn and the price of manufactures, with regard to natural or necessary price, is this; that if the price of any manufacture were essentially depressed, the whole manufacture would be entirely destroyed; whereas, if the price of corn were essentially depressed, the *quantity* of it only would be diminished. There would be some machinery in the country still capable of sending the commodity to market at the reduced price.

The earth has been sometimes compared to a vast machine, presented by nature to man for the production of food and raw materials; but, to make the resemblance more just, as far as they admit of comparison, we should consider the soil as a present to man of a great number of machines, all susceptible of continued improvement by the application of capital to them, but yet of very different original qualities and powers.

This great inequality in the powers of the machinery employed in procuring raw produce, forms one of the most remarkable features which distinguishes the machinery of the land from the machinery employed in manufactures.

When a machine in manufactures is invented, which will produce more finished work with less labour and capital than before, if there be no patent, or as soon as the patent is over, a sufficient number of such machines may be made to supply the whole demand, and to supersede entirely the use of all the old machinery. The natural consequence is, that the price is reduced to the price of production from the best machinery, and if the price were to be depressed lower, the whole of the commodity would be withdrawn from the market.

The machines which produce corn and raw materials on the contrary, are the gifts of nature, not the works of man; and we find, by experience, that these gifts have very different qualities and powers. The most fertile lands of a country, those which, like the best machinery in manufactures, yield the greatest products with the least labour and capital, are never found sufficient to supply the effective demand of an increasing population. The price of raw produce, therefore, naturally rises till it becomes sufficiently high to pay the cost of raising it with inferior machines, and by a more expensive process; and, as there cannot be two prices for corn of the same quality, all the other machines, the working of which requires less capital compared with the produce, must yield rents in proportion to their goodness.

Every extensive country may thus be considered as possessing a gradation of machines for the production of corn and raw materials, including in this gradation not only all the various qualities of poor land, of which every large territory has generally an abundance, but the inferior machinery which may be said to be employed when good land is further and further forced for additional produce. As the price of raw produce continues to rise, these inferior machines are successively called into action; and, as the price of raw produce continues to fall, they are successively thrown out of action. The illustration here used serves to shew at once the necessity of the actual price of corn to the actual produce, and the different effect which would attend a great reduction in the price of any particular manufacture, and a great reduction in the price of raw produce.

I hope to be excused for dwelling a little, and presenting to the reader in various forms the doctrine, that corn in reference to the *quantity actually produced* is sold at its necessary price like manufactures, because I consider it as a truth of the highest importance, which has been entirely overlooked by the Economists, by Adam Smith, and all those writers who have represented raw produce as selling always at a monopoly price.

Adam Smith has very clearly explained in what manner the progress of wealth and improvement tends to raise the price of cattle, poultry, the materials of clothing and lodging, the most useful minerals, &c. &c. compared with corn ; but he has not entered into the explanation of the natural causes which tend to determine the price of corn. He has left the reader, indeed, to conclude, that he considers the price of corn as determined only by the state of the mines which at the time supply the circulating medium of the commercial world. But this is a cause obviously inadequate to account for the actual differences in the price of grain, observable in countries at no great distance from each other, and at nearly the same distance from the mines.

I entirely agree with him, that it is of great use to enquire into the causes of high price; as, from the result of such inquiry, it may turn out, that the very circumstance of which we complain, may be the necessary consequence and the most certain sign of increasing wealth and prosperity. But, of all inquiries of this kind, none surely can be so important, or so generally interesting, as an inquiry into the causes which affect the price of corn, and which occasion the differences in this price, so observable in different countries.

I have no hesitation in stating that, independently of irregularities in the currency of a country,* and other temporary and accidental

---

* In all our discussions we should endeavour, as well as

circumstances, the cause of the high comparative money price of corn is its high comparative real price, or the greater quantity of capital and labour which must be employed to produce it: and that the reason why the real price of corn is higher and continually rising in countries which are already rich, and still advancing in prosperity and population, is to be found in the necessity of resorting constantly to poorer land—to machines which require a greater expenditure to work them—and which consequently occasion each fresh addition to the raw produce of the country to be purchased at a greater cost—in short, it is to be found in the important truth that corn, in a *progressive country*, is sold at the price necessary to yield the actual supply; and that, as this supply becomes more and more difficult, the price rises in proportion.*

---

we can, to separate that part of high price, which arises from excess of currency, from that part, which is natural, and arises from permanent causes. In the whole course of this argument, it is particularly necessary to do this.

* It will be observed, that I have said in a *progressive country ;* that is, in a country which requires yearly the employment of a greater capital on the land, to support an increasing population. If there were no question about fresh capital, or an increase of people, and all the land were

The price of corn, as determined by these causes, will of course be greatly modified by other circumstances; by direct and indirect taxation; by improvements in the modes of cultivation; by the saving of labour on the land; and particularly by the importations of foreign corn. The latter cause, indeed, may do away, in a considerable degree, the usual effects of great wealth on the price of corn; and this wealth will then shew itself in a different form.

Let us suppose seven or eight large countries not very distant from each other, and not very differently situated with regard to the mines. Let us suppose further, that neither their soils nor their skill in agriculture are essentially unlike; that their currencies are in a natural state; their taxes nothing; and that every trade is free, except the trade in corn.

---

good, it would not then be true that corn must be sold at its necessary price. The actual price might be diminished; and if the rents of land were diminished in proportion, the cultivation might go on as before, and the same quantity be produced. It very rarely happens, however, that all the lands of a country actually occupied are good, and yield a good neat rent. And in all cases, a fall of prices must destroy agricultural capital during the currency of leases; and on their renewal there would not be the same power of production.

I et us now suppose one of them very greatly
to increase in capital and manufacturing skill
above the rest, and to become in consequence
much more rich and populous. I should say,
that this great comparative increase of riches
could not possibly take place, without a great
comparative advance in the price of raw produce; and that such advance of price would,
under the circumstances supposed, be the natural sign and absolutely necessary consequence, of the increased wealth and population
of the country in question.

Let us now suppose the same countries to
have the most perfect freedom of intercourse
in corn, and the expenses of freight, &c. to be
quite inconsiderable. And let us still suppose
one of them to increase very greatly above the
rest, in manufacturing capital and skill, in
wealth and population. I should then say,
that as the importation of corn would prevent
any great difference in the price of raw produce, it would prevent any great difference in
the quantity of capital laid out upon the land,
and the quantity of corn obtained from it;
that, consequently, the great increase of wealth
could not take place without a great dependence on the other nations for corn; and that
this dependence, under the circumstances supposed, would be the natural sign, and absolutely

necessary consequence of the increased wealth and population of the country in question.

These I consider as the two alternatives necessarily belonging to a great comparative increase of wealth; and the supposition here made will, with proper restrictions, apply to the state of Europe.

In Europe, the expenses attending the carriage of corn are often considerable. They form a natural barrier to importation; and even the country which habitually depends upon foreign corn, must have the price of its raw produce considerably higher than the general level. Practically, also, the prices of raw produce, in the different countries of Europe, will be variously modified by very different soils, very different degrees of taxation, and very different degrees of improvement in the science of agriculture. Heavy taxation, and a poor soil, may occasion a high comparative price of raw produce, or a considerable dependance on other countries, without great wealth and population; while great improvements in agriculture and a good soil may keep the price of produce low, and the country independent of foreign corn, in spite of considerable wealth. But the principles laid down are the general principles on the subject; and in applying them to any particular case, the particular circumstances of such case must always be taken into the consideration.

With regard to improvements in agriculture, which in similar soils is the great cause which retards the advance of price compared with the advance of produce; although they are sometimes very powerful, they are rarely found sufficient to balance the necessity of applying to poorer land, or inferior machines. In this respect, raw produce is essentially different from manufactures.

The real price of manufactures, the quantity of labour and capital necessary to produce a given quantity of them, is almost constantly diminishing; while the quantity of labour and capital, necessary to procure the last addition that has been made to the raw produce of a rich and advancing country, is almost constantly increasing. We see in consequence, that in spite of continued improvements in agriculture, the money price of corn is *cœteris paribus* the highest in the richest countries, while in spite of this high price of corn, and consequent high price of labour, the money price of manufactures still continues lower than in poorer countries.

I cannot then agree with Adam Smith, in thinking that the low value of gold and silver is no proof of the wealth and flourishing state of the country, where it takes place. Nothing of course can be inferred from it, taken absolutely, except the abundance of the mines; but taken relatively, or in comparison with the state of other countries, much may be inferred from it. If we are to measure the value of the precious metals in different countries, and at different periods in the same country, by the price of corn and labour, which appears to me to be the nearest practical approximation that can be adopted (and in fact corn is the measure used by Adam Smith himself), it appears to me to follow, that in countries which have a frequent commercial intercourse with each other, which are nearly at the same distance from the mines, and are not essentially different in soil; there is no more certain sign, or more necessary consequence of superiority of wealth, than the low value of the precious metals, or the high price of raw produce.*

---

* This conclusion may appear to contradict the doctrine of the *level* of the precious metals. And so it does, if by *level* be meant level of value estimated in the usual way. I consider the doctrine, indeed, as quite unsupported by facts, and the comparison of the precious metals to water perfectly inaccurate. The precious metals are always tending to a state of rest, or such a state of things as to make their movement unnecessary. But when this state of rest has been nearly attained, and the exchanges of all countries are nearly at par, the value of the precious metals in different

It is of importance to ascertain this point; that we may not complain of one of the most certain proofs of the prosperous condition of a country.

It is not of course meant to be asserted, that the high price of raw produce is, separately taken, advantageous to the consumer; but that it is the necessary concomitant of superior and increasing wealth, and that one of them cannot be had without the other.*

With regard to the labouring classes of society, whose interests as consumers may be supposed to be most nearly concerned, it is a very short-sighted view of the subject, which contemplates, with alarm, the high price of corn as certainly injurious to them. The essentials to their well being are their own prudential ha-

---

countries, estimated in corn and labour, or the mass of commodities, is very far indeed from being the same. To be convinced of this, it is only necessary to look at England, France, Poland, Russia, and India, when the exchanges are at par. That Adam Smith, who proposes labour as the true measure of value at all times and in all places, could look around him, and yet say that the precious metals were always the highest in value in the richest countries, has always appeared to me most unlike his usual attention to found his theories on facts.

* Even upon the system of importation, in the actual state and situation of the countries of Europe, higher prices must accompany superior and increasing wealth.

bits, and the *increasing demand* for labour. And I do no scruple distinctly to affirm, that under similar habits, and a similar demand for labour, the high price of corn, when it has had time to produce its natural effects, so far from being a disadvantage to them, is a positive and unquestionable advantage. To supply the same demand for labour, the necessary price of production must be paid, and they must be able to command the same quantities of the necessaries of life, whether they are high or low in price.* But if they are able to com-

---

* We must not be so far deceived by the evidence before Parliament, relating to the want of connexion between the prices of corn and of labour, as to suppose that they are really independent of each other. The price of the necessaries of life is, in fact, the cost of producing labour. The supply cannot proceed, if it be not paid; and though there will always be a little latitude, owing to some variations of industry and habits, and the distance of time between the encouragement to population and the period of the results appearing in the markets: yet it is a still greater error, to suppose the price of labour unconnected with the price of corn, than to suppose that the price of corn immediately and completely regulates it. Corn and labour rarely march quite abreast; but there is an obvious limit, beyond which they cannot be separated. With regard to the unusual exertions made by the labouring classes in periods of dearness, which produce the fall of wages noticed in the evidence, they are most meritorious in the individuals, and certainly favour the growth of capital. But no man of humanity could

mand the same quantity of necessaries, and receive a money price for their labour, proportioned to their advanced price, there is no doubt that, with regard to all the objects of convenience and comfort, which do not rise in proportion to corn, (and there are many such consumed by the poor) their condition will be most decidedly improved.

The reader will observe in what manner I have guarded the proposition. I am well aware, and indeed have myself stated in another place, that the price of provisions often rises, without a proportionate rise of labour: but this cannot possibly happen for any length of time, if the *demand for labour* continues increasing at the same rate, and the habits of the labourer are not altered, either with regard to

---

wish to see them constant and unremitted. They are most admirable as a temporary relief; but if they were constantly in action, effects of a similar kind would result from them, as from the population of a country being pushed to the very extreme limits of its food. There would be no resources in a scarcity. I own I do not see, with pleasure, the great extension of the practice of task work. To work really hard during twelve or fourteen hours in the day, for any length of time, is too much for a human being. Some intervals of ease are necessary to health and happiness: and the occasional abuse of such intervals is no valid argument against their use.

prudence, or the quantity of work which he is disposed to perform.

The peculiar evil to be apprehended is, that the high money price of labour may diminish the demand for it; and that it has this tendency will be readily allowed, particularly as it tends to increase the prices of exportable commodities. But repeated experience has shewn us that such tendencies are continually counter balanced, and more than counter balanced by other circumstances. And we have witnessed, in our own country, a greater and more rapid extension of foreign commerce, than perhaps was ever known, under the apparent disadvantage of a very great increase in the price of corn and labour, compared with the prices of surrounding countries.

On the other hand, instances every where abound of a very low money price of labour, totally failing to produce an increasing demand for it. And among the labouring classes of different countries, none certainly are so wretched as those, where the demand for labour, and the population are stationary, and yet the prices of provisions extremely low, compared with manufactures and foreign commodities. However low they may be, it is certain, that under such circumstances, no more will fall to the share of the labourer than is necessary just to maintain the actual population; and his condition will be depressed, not only by the stationary demand for labour, but by the additional evil of being able to command but a small portion of manufactures or foreign commodities, with the little surplus which he may possess. If, for instance, under a stationary population, we suppose, that in average families two-thirds of the wages estimated in corn are spent in necessary provisions, it will make a great difference in the condition of the poor, whether the remaining one-third will command few or many conveniencies and comforts; and almost invariably, the higher is the price of corn, the more indulgences will a given surplus purchase.

The high or low price of provisions, therefore, in any country is evidently a most uncertain criterion of the state of the poor in that country. Their condition obviously depends upon other more powerful causes; and it is probably true, that it is as frequently good, or perhaps more frequently so, in countries where corn is high, than where it is low.

At the same time it should be observed, that the high price of corn, occasioned by the difficulty of procuring it, may be considered as the ultimate check to the indefinite progress of a country in wealth and population. And, although the actual progress of countries be subject to great variations in their rate of movement, both from external and internal causes, and it would be rash to say that a state which is well peopled and proceeding rather slowly at present, may not proceed rapidly forty years hence; yet it must be owned, that the chances of a future rapid progress are diminished by the high prices of corn and labour, compared with other countries.

It is, therefore, of great importance, that these prices should be increased as little as possible artificially, that is, by taxation. But every tax which falls upon agricultural capital tends to check the application of such capital, to the bringing of fresh land under cultivation, and the improvement of the old. It was shewn, in a former part of this inquiry, that before such application of capital could take place, the price of produce, compared with the instruments of production, must rise sufficiently to pay the farmer. But, if the increasing difficulties to be overcome are aggravated by taxation, it is necessary, that before the proposed improvements are undertaken, the price should rise sufficiently, not only to pay the farmer, but also the government. And every tax, which falls on agricultural capital, either prevents a proposed improvement, or causes it to be purchased at a higher price.

When new leases are let, these taxes are generally thrown off upon the landlord. The farmer so makes his bargain, or ought so to make it, as to leave himself, after every expense has been paid, the average profits of agricultural stock in the actual circumstances of the country, whatever they may be, and in whatever manner they may have been affected by taxes, particularly by so general a one as the property tax. The farmer, therefore, by paying a less rent to his landlord on the renewal of his lease, is relieved from any peculiar pressure, and may go on in the common routine of cultivation with the common profits. But his encouragement to lay out fresh capital in improvements is by no means restored by his new bargain. This encouragement must depend, both with regard to the farmer and the landlord himself, exclusively on the price of produce, compared with the price of the instruments of production; and, if the price of these instruments have been raised by taxation, no diminution of rent can give relief. It is, in fact, a question, in which rent is not concerned. And, with a view to *progressive improvements*, it may be safely asserted, that the total abolition of rents would be less effectual than the removal of taxes which fall upon agricultural capital.

I believe it to be the prevailing opinion, that the great expense of growing corn in this country is almost exclusively owing to the weight of taxation. Of the tendency of many of our taxes to increase the expenses of cultivation and the price of corn, I feel no doubt; but the reader will see from the course of argument pursued in this inquiry, that I think a part of this price, and perhaps no inconsiderable part, arises from a cause which lies deeper, and is in fact the necessary result of the great superiority of our wealth and population, compared with the quality of our natural soil and the extent of our territory.

This is a cause which can only be essentially mitigated by the habitual importation of foreign corn, and a diminished cultivation of it at home. The policy of such a system has been discussed in another place; but, of course, every relief from taxation must tend, under any system, to make the price of corn less high, and importation less necessary.

In the progress of a country towards a high state of improvement, the positive wealth of the landlord ought, upon the principles which have been laid down, gradually to increase; although his relative condition and influence in society will probably rather diminish, owing to the increasing number and wealth of those who live upon a still more important surplus*—the profits of stock.

The progressive fall, with few exceptions, in the value of the precious metals throughout Europe; the still greater fall, which has occurred in the richest countries, together with the increase of produce which has been obtained from the soil, must all conduce to make the landlord expect an increase of rents on the renewal of his leases. But, in re-letting his farms, he is liable to fall into two errors, which are almost equally prejudicial to his own interests, and to those of his country.

In the first place, he may be induced, by the immediate prospect of an exorbitant rent, offered by farmers bidding against each other, to let his land to a tenant without sufficient capital to cultivate it in the best way, and make the necessary improvements upon it. This is undoubtedly a most short-sighted policy, the bad effects of which have been strongly noticed

---

* I have hinted before, in a note, that profits may, without impropriety, be called a surplus. But, whether surplus or not, they are the most important source of wealth, as they are, beyond all question, the main source of accumulation.

by the most intelligent land surveyors in the evidence lately brought before Parliament; and have been particularly remarkable in Ireland, where the imprudence of the landlords in this respect, combined, perhaps, with some real difficulty of finding substantial tenants, has aggravated the discontents of the country, and thrown the most serious obstacles in the way of an improved system of cultivation. The consequence of this error is the certain loss of all that future source of rent to the landlord, and wealth to the country, which arises from increase of produce.

The second error to which the landlord is liable, is that of mistaking a mere temporary rise of prices, for a rise of sufficient duration to warrant an increase of rents. It frequently happens, that a scarcity of one or two years, or an unusual demand arising from any other cause, may raise the price of raw produce to a height, at which it cannot be maintained. And the farmers, who take land under the influence of such prices, will, in the return of a mere natural state of things, probably break, and leave their farms in a ruined and exhausted state. These short periods of high price are of great importance in generating capital upon the land, if the farmers are allowed to have the advantage of them; but, if they are grasped at prematurely by the landlord, capital is destroyed, instead of being accumulated; and both the landlord and the country incur a loss, instead of gaining a benefit.

A similar caution is necessary in raising rents, even when the rise of prices seems as if it would be permanent. In the progress of prices and rents, rent ought always to be a little behind; not only to afford the means of ascertaining whether the rise be temporary or permanent, but even in the latter case, to give a little time for the accumulation of capital on the land, of which the landholder is sure to feel the full benefit in the end.

There is no just reason to believe, that if the lands were to give the whole of their rents to their t nants, corn would be more plentiful and cheaper. If the view of the subject, taken in the preceding inquiry, be correct, the last additions made to our home produce are sold at the cost of production, and the same quantity could not be produced from our own soil at a less price, even without rent. The effect of transferring all rents to tenants, would be merely the turning them into gentlemen, and tempting them to cultivate their farms under the superintendance of careless and uninterested bailiffs, instead of the vigilant eye of a master, who is deterred from carelessness by the fear

of ruin, and stimulated to exertion by the hope
of a competence. The most numerous instances of successful industry, and well directed
knowledge, have been found among those who
have paid a fair rent for their lands; who have
embarked the whole of their capital in their
undertaking; and who feel it their duty to
watch over it with unceasing care, and add to
it whenever it is possible. But when this
laudable spirit prevails among a tenantry, it is
of the very utmost importance to the progress
of riches, and the permanent increase of rents,
that it should have the power as well as the
will to accumulate; and an interval of advancing prices, not immediately followed by
a proportionate rise of rents, furnishes the most
effective powers of this kind. These intervals
of advancing prices, when not succeeded by
retrograde movements, most powerfully con-
tribute to the progress of national wealth.
And practically I should say, that when once
a character of industry and economy has been
established, temporary high profits are a more
frequent and powerful source of accumulation,
than either an increased spirit of saving, or
any other cause that can be named.* It is the

---

* Adam Smith notices the bad effects of high profits on
the habits of the capitalist. They may perhaps sometimes

only cause which seems capable of accounting for the prodigious accumulation among individuals, which must have taken place in this country during the last twenty years, and which has left us with a greatly increased capital, notwithstanding our vast annual destruction of stock, for so long a period.

Among the temporary causes of high price, which may sometimes mislead the landlord, it is necessary to notice irregularities in the currency. When they are likely to be of short duration, they must be treated by the landlord in the same manner as years of unusual demand. But when they continue so long as they have done in this country, it is impossible for the landlord to do otherwise than proportion his rent accordingly, and take the chance of being obliged to lessen it again, on the return of the currency to its natural state.

The present fall in the price of bullion, and the improved state of our exchanges, proves, in my opinion. that a much greater part of the difference between gold and paper was owing to commercial causes, and a peculiar demand

---

occasion extravagance; but generally, I should say, that extravagant habits were a more frequent cause of a scarcity of capital and high profits, than high profits of extravagant habits.

for bullion than was supposed by many persons; but they by no means prove that the issue of paper did not allow of a higher rise of prices than could be permanently maintained. Already a retrograde movement, not exclusively occasioned by the importations of corn, has been sensibly felt; and it must go somewhat further before we can return to payments in specie. Those who let their lands during the period of the greatest difference between notes and bullion, must probably lower them, whichever system may be adopted with regard to the trade in corn. These retrograde movements are always unfortunate; and high rents, partly occasioned by causes of this kind, greatly embarrass the regular march of prices, and confound the calculations both of the farmer and landlord.

With the cautions here noticed in letting farms, the landlord may fairly look forward to a gradual and permanent increase of rents; and, in general, not only to an increase proportioned to the rise in the *price* of produce, but to a still further increase, arising from an increase in the *quantity* of produce.

If in taking rents, which are equally fair for the landlord and tenant, it is found that in successive lettings they do not rise rather more than in proportion to the price of produce, it will generally be owing to heavy taxation.

Though it is by no means true, as stated by the Economists, that all taxes fall on the neat rents of the landlords, yet it is certainly true that they are more frequently taxed both indirectly as well as directly, and have less power of relieving themselves, than any other order of the state. And as they pay, as they certainly do, many of the taxes which fall on the capital of the farmer and the wages of the labourer, as well as those directly imposed on themselves; they must necessarily feel it in the diminution of that portion of the whole produce, which under other circumstances would have fallen to their share. But the degree in which the different classes of society are affected by taxes, is in itself a copious subject, belonging to the general principles of taxation, and deserves a separate inquiry.

THE END.